Those Giant Giraffes

Those Giant Giraffes

Jan Lee Wicker

Illustrations by Steve Weaver

Pineapple Press, Inc.

Sarasota, Florida

Inquiries should be addressed to:
Pineapple Press, Inc.
P.O. Box 3889
Sarasota, Florida 34230

www.pineapplepress.com

Photo Credits

Cover © Tangsanshi/Dreamstime.com; page 2 © Mikeofthethomas/Dreamstime.com; page 5 © Paul Van Eykelen/Dreamstime.com; page 8, Paul Wicker; page 10 © Sergey Uryadnikov/Dreamstime.com; page 12 © Vchphoto/Dreamstime.com; page 14 © Ali Taylor/Dreamstime.com; page 18 © Roman Murushkin/Dreamstime.com; page 20 © Antonella865/Dreamstime.com; page 22 © Luisrsphoto/Dreamstime.com; page 24 © Dennis Donohue/Dreamstime.com; page 26 © Clearviewstock/Dreamstime.com; page 28 © Steve Allen/Dreamstime.com; page 30 © Ccat82/Dreamstime.com; page 34 © Timbooth2770/Dreamstime.com; page 36 © Brandon Alms/Dreamstime.com; page 38 © Nick Biemans/Dreamstime.com; page 40 © Henkbentlage/Dreamstime.com; page 42, Meagan Wicker (Lazy 5 Ranch); page 44 © Nomisg/Dreamstime.com; page 46 © Mogens Trolle/Dreamstime.com; pages 48–50, Jan Wicker; page 52 top © Roman Murushkin/Dreamstime.com; page 52 bottom © Steve Allen/Dreamstime.com; page 53 top left © Clearviewstock/Dreamstime.com; page 53 top right © Timbooth2770/Dreamstime.com; page 53 bottom left © Christophe D./Dreamstime.com; page 53 bottom right © Pavboq/Dreamstime.com; page 54, Chris Wicker

Library of Congress Cataloging-in-Publication Data

Wicker, Jan Lee.
Those giant giraffes / Jan Lee Wicker. — First edition.
pages cm
Audience: Ages 5 to 9.
Audience: Grades K to 3.
ISBN 978-1-56164-788-0 (pbk. : alk. paper)
1. Giraffe—Juvenile literature. I. Title.

QL737.U56W56 2015
599.638—dc23
2015001152

First Edition
10 9 8 7 6 5 4 3 2 1

Printed in the United States

To Hannah, who loves animals

CONTENTS

How tall are giraffes?

Giraffes are the tallest animals on land. Full-grown giraffes are from 15 to 18 feet tall. That means a giraffe can be taller than 3 women standing on top of each other. The tallest giraffe ever found was a male 19 feet tall. A giraffe's neck is about 6 ½ feet long. A giraffe could look into a second-story window with ease.

How giant are giraffes?

Besides being tall, a giraffe is a giant in many ways. A giraffe's heart can weigh up to 24 pounds and is 2 feet long. Its size allows the blood to be pumped throughout their tall bodies. They have the longest tails of any animal. The whole tail is about 6 feet long, including the 3-foot-long tassel on the end. Giraffes can weigh up to 4000 pounds (as much as a large car). A giraffe's hoofprint is as big as a dinner plate (1 foot wide). Each giraffe step measures 15 feet. An adult human would have to take 6 steps for every one giraffe step.

Why do giraffes have long tongues?

A giraffe's long tongue helps it to eat the leaves of tall trees. Their tongues are dark blue and very wet. The dark color is like natural sunscreen. It keeps their tongues from being sunburned while they eat. A giraffe's tongue can be 20 inches long. That is as long as a child's arm.

How fast can a giraffe run?

A giraffe can gallop up to 35 miles an hour. That is faster than a car goes in town. When they run, their front legs do most of the pushing. That is why they have such large muscles in their shoulders. When they walk they swing both legs on the same side of the body at the same time. When they run, they move the back legs and then the front ones.

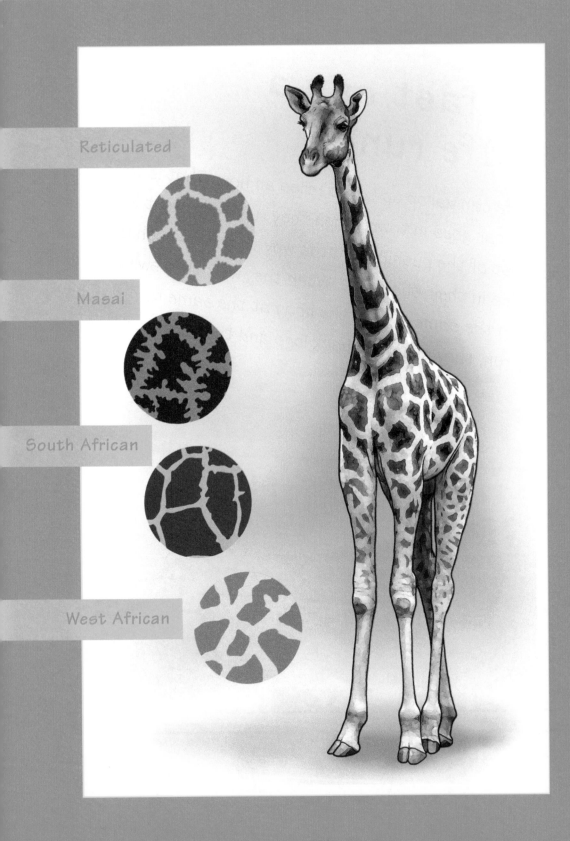

Reticulated

Masai

South African

West African

How many different kinds of giraffes are there?

There is only one species or kind of giraffe. There are 9 different subspecies. They are the Angolan, Kordofan, Masai, Nubian, Reticulated, Rothschild's, South African, Thornicroft's, and the West African. You can usually tell one kind from another by the different size, shape, and color of their spots.

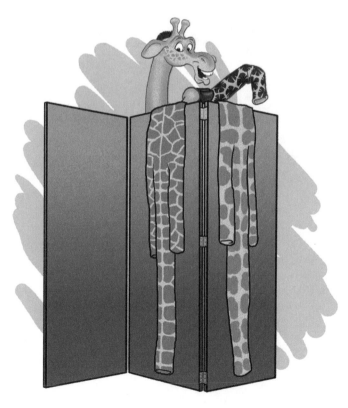

Are giraffes endangered?

Yes. The West African and the Rothschild's giraffes are both endangered. One reason is poaching (illegal hunting for their meat, coats, and tails). Another reason is loss of habitat because of the growth of human population near them. There are only 80,000 giraffes left in the wild. Of these, there are only 670 Rothschild's and only 250 West African giraffes left. The giraffe is in danger and must be protected.

Why do giraffes have spots?

The giraffe's skin pattern helps it hide in the trees. Their spots help camouflage giraffes so it is harder for lions and other predators to see them. A giraffe may look like a tall dead tree from a distance. Looking like a tree can save your life if a lion is after you!

How many horns do giraffes have?

The "horns" on a giraffe are not really horns. They are bony lumps on the skull. They are covered with hair and skin. Giraffes can have up to 5 of these lumps or ossicones. A baby giraffe is born with these lumps flat on its head. Within the first week of life they pop upright.

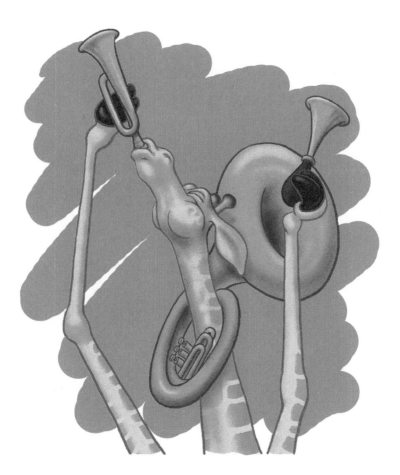

Do giraffes live in groups?

Yes. These groups are called herds. Some herds are made up of all cows (females) and their calves (babies). Other herds are all young bulls (males). There are usually 12–15 giraffes in a herd. Only the older bulls live alone. They wander from herd to herd.

What do giraffes eat?

Giraffes are vegetarians. They eat up to 140 pounds of leaves a day. Many of these leaves have long thorns on them. The giraffes are able to eat these thorny leaves by producing thick saliva to help them swallow the thorns. A male eats the leaves by stretching up tall. The females usually bend their necks to eat the lower leaves. That way the males and females aren't fighting over the same leaves. Giraffes also eat seeds, flowers, and fruit.

27

How do giraffes drink water?

Giraffes don't have to drink water very often since they get most of their water from their food. When they have to drink at a water hole, they have to spread their legs apart and bend their knees in order to drink. They can drink 10 gallons of water at one time.

Is a giraffe kin to camels or horses?

No, but they are similar. Giraffes do have hooves like a horse. And, like camels, they don't have to drink a lot of water. The giraffe's closest relative is an okapi. The okapi lives in dense forest in central Africa. It is shorter than a giraffe, with zebra-like stripes on its legs, and it has a dark brown coat of fur.

Africa

South Atlantic Ocean

Indian Ocean

Where in the world do giraffes live?

They only live on the continent of Africa. They are found as far north as Chad and all the way down to South Africa. They are found as far west as Niger and as far east as Somalia. Giraffes from different parts of Africa have different patterns on their skin. Scientists think it may have to do with the types of plants available in the different areas.

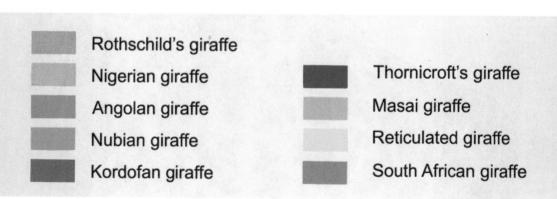

- Rothschild's giraffe
- Nigerian giraffe
- Angolan giraffe
- Nubian giraffe
- Kordofan giraffe
- Thornicroft's giraffe
- Masai giraffe
- Reticulated giraffe
- South African giraffe

Do males and females look alike?

The easiest way to tell males from females is by looking at their horns. The males have larger horns than the females. The horns on the males usually have little hair on them since they use them to fight and the hair gets rubbed off. Young males still have hair on their horns. Usually males are taller and weigh more than females.

Do giraffes make noise?

Although they can grunt, snort, growl, and cough, giraffes don't make noises very often. They have been heard to moo like a cow or make sounds like a bull or calf. Even though they are mostly quiet, their snoring could wake you up.

How big are baby giraffes?

A baby giraffe weighs about 100–150 pounds and is 6 feet tall when it is born. At birth, the baby falls 6 feet to the ground since the mother has her baby while standing up. When the calf is just one hour old, it can stand up, walk, and run. Giraffes usually have one baby at a time.

Do giraffes have any enemies?

Yes. Lions, leopards, African wild dogs, and packs of hyenas are their enemies. More than half of the giraffe calves become prey to these enemies. An adult giraffe can kill a lion just by kicking it. Giraffes only sleep 5–30 minutes a day. This allows them to constantly be on the lookout for enemies. Although the giraffes can sit down by bending their legs underneath their bodies, they rarely sit in the wild. Once they sit down, they can't stand up very fast.

Can you hand-feed giraffes?

Yes, many zoos give you a chance to feed a giraffe. The giraffe uses its long blue tongue to eat the food out of your hand. Your hand will be wet with saliva, but it's worth it! It is amazing to watch their tongues. They will also eat food out of buckets that you hold. Either way, it is an experience that you won't forget.

Why are there birds on a giraffe's neck?

The oxpecker is the name of the bird that you often see on hippos, zebras, and other large mammals in the wild, including giraffes. The giraffe and the oxpecker both benefit from this relationship. While the oxpecker gets a free meal of ticks, the giraffe gets rid of ticks. These ticks suck the blood from the giraffe's neck and carry diseases.

Do giraffes fight?

Yes. The males use their horns and heads to fight with each other. They do this to decide which is the stronger male. They also compete by "necking." Necking is when giraffes use their necks to wrestle, just like boys might arm wrestle with one another to see who is the strongest.

Activities

Giraffe Frame Game

Material needed:
brown paper, white sheet of paper, blue and black crayons

1. Draw a window frame.
2. Draw two diagonal lines to represent the giraffe's neck.
3. Color the window frame.
4. Cut out brown shapes to become the giraffe's patterns.
5. Glue the shapes on the giraffe's neck.
6. Color in the sky background for the giraffe.
7. Now you have a giraffe walking by a tall window.

Graham Cracker Giraffe

Material needed:

4 stick pretzels, 1 large graham cracker, icing or cream cheese, 1 black M&M, several pieces of Cinnamon Toast Crunch cereal, red licorice that can be pulled apart in strings.

1. Break the cracker so that there is one large square and two thin rectangles.
2. Break one thin rectangle in half for the head.
3. Spread icing on the large square (body), on one thin long rectangle (neck), and on the short rectangle (head).
4. Arrange the crackers to look like the body, neck, and head.
5. Add the M&M for the eye.
6. Place the 4 pretzels as legs.
7. Place the cereal pieces on the body and neck to be the patches on the giraffe's body.

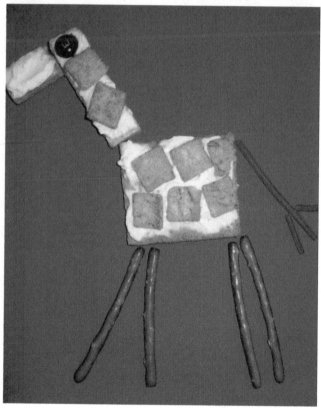

8. Add the red licorice tail. Pull apart one long string for the tail.
9. Pull another string off and tear it up into smaller pieces for the tassel of hair on the end of the tail.
10. Look at your cute giraffe and eat it up!

Handprint Giraffe

Material needed:
paper or fabric to work on, white or yellow paint, black paint and brown or colorful paint (with a tip), Q-tip, toothpick. (Use fabric paint if you work on fabric.)

1. Paint your whole hand (including your 4 fingers but not your thumb) white or yellow.
2. Press it on the paper (or fabric) with your 4 fingers pointed to the bottom. These are the 4 legs.
3. Paint the side of your hand, from the tip of your pinky up to where your palm ends.
4. Press it up at one of the top corners of the giraffe's body. This is the neck.
5. Paint your thumb and add it at the end of the neck for the head. Face it pointing away from the body, with the fingernail end as the rounded end of the head.
6. Put your fingertip in the brown paint and give your giraffe 4 hoof feet.
7. Using the brown tip paint, outline the giraffe's body.
8. Then draw a tail (with tassel), a mouth, one nostril, one ear, and two horns.
9. Add one eye using black paint with a Q-tip.
10. Squirt a line of paint from the head and down the neck. Then use a toothpick to make the mane shaggy.
11. Finally, use a Q-tip to add the patches to your giraffe.

Where to Learn More about Giraffes

Good Books to Read

Giraffes by Catherine Ipcizade, Capstone Press, Minnesota, 2008.

Giraffes by Sally Morgan, Teacher Created Resources, California, 2006.

Zoobooks: Giraffes by John Bonnett Wexo, Wildlife Education, California, 2005.

Good Websites to Visit

www.animalfactguide.com

www.lazy5ranch.com

www.nationalgeographickids.com

video.nationalgeographic.com
  Look at the video "Lives of Giraffes."

Glossary

bull – a male giraffe (also the male of other mammals such as dolphins, moose, elephants)

calf – a young male or female of a giraffe, dolphin, moose, elephant, etc.

camouflage – a natural coloring that helps an animal hide and blend into its habitat

coat – the fur and design of a giraffe

continent – one of the seven large land areas on Earth. Africa is one of them.

cow – the adult female of many mammals, including giraffes

dense – crowded together

endangered – when an animal is in danger of becoming extinct or dying off

habitat – the place where an animal lives

herd – a group of animals that live together

hooves – the hard foot coverings of a giraffe and some other animals

hyena – a wild animal in Africa that looks like a large dog and is a predator of giraffes

illegal – against the law

natural – not man-made

necking – when giraffes use their necks to fight or show affection

ossicones – the pair of hard growths on a giraffe's head, often referred to as horns

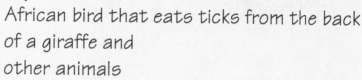

oxpecker – the African bird that eats ticks from the back of a giraffe and other animals

poaching – illegal hunting for a giraffe's meat, coat, and tail

population – the total number of people or animals that live in an area

predators – animals that eat other animals

prey – animals that are eaten by other animals

saliva – the watery liquid that is found in the mouth of animals that helps with digestion

species – a type of plant or animal

tassel – the group of hairs found at the end of a giraffe's tail

About the Author

Jan Lee Wicker has taught children in pre-school through first grade for more than 30 years. From the first time she hand-fed a giraffe, she knew she wanted to write a book about giraffes. She is pictured with one of the giraffes from the Lazy 5 Ranch in Mooresville, NC. She and her husband have two grown sons. She has also written *Those Funny Flamingos, Those Excellent Eagles, Those Delightful Dolphins, Those Magical Manatees* and *Those Big Bears.*

Index

Photographs are indicated by **boldface** type.

Here are the other books in this series. For a complete catalog, visit our website at www.pineapplepress.com.

Those Amazing Alligators by Kathy Feeney. Discover the differences between alligators and crocodiles. Learn what alligators eat, how they communicate, and much more.

Those Beautiful Butterflies by Sarah Cussen. Learn all about butterflies—their behavior, why they look the way they do, how they communicate, and why they love bright flowers.

Those Big Bears by Jan Lee Wicker. Why do bears stand on two legs? How do they use their claws? How many kinds are there? What do they do all winter?

Those Colossal Cats by Marta Magellan. Meet lions, tigers, leopards, and the other big cats. Do they purr? How fast can they run? Which is biggest?

Those Delightful Dolphins by Jan Lee Wicker. Dolphins are delightful in the way they communicate and play with one another and the way they cooperate with humans.

Those Enormous Elephants by Sarah Cussen. Sure they are the biggest land animals, but what else is unique about elephants? Why do they have tusks and trunks?

Those Excellent Eagles by Jan Lee Wicker. Learn all about those excellent eagles—what they eat, how fast they fly, why the American bald eagle is our nation's national bird.

Those Funny Flamingos by Jan Lee Wicker. Why are these funny birds pink? Why do they stand on one leg and eat upside down? Where do they live?

Those Kooky Kangaroos by Bonnie Nickel. Kangaroos don't look like other animals, they don't walk like other animals, and their babies are very peculiar.

Those Lively Lizards by Marta Magellan. Meet lizards that can run on water, some with funny-looking eyes, some that change color, and some that look like little dinosaurs.

Those Magical Manatees by Jan Lee Wicker. Why are they magical? How big are they? What do they eat? Why are they endangered and what can you do to help?

Those Mischievous Monkeys by Bonnie Nickel. Find out where in the world monkeys live, what they eat, and what they do for fun.

Those Outrageous Owls by Laura Wyatt. Learn what owls eat, how they hunt, and why they look the way they do. How do they fly so quietly? Why do horned owls have horns?

Those Peculiar Pelicans by Sarah Cussen. Find out how much food those peculiar pelicans can fit in their beaks, how they stay cool, and whether they really steal fish from fishermen.

Those Perky Penguins by Sarah Cussen. Can penguins fly? Do they get cold? How many kinds are there and where in the world do they live?

Those Terrific Turtles by Sarah Cussen. You'll learn the difference between a turtle and a tortoise, and find out why they have shells. Meet baby turtles and some very, very old ones.

Those Voracious Vultures by Marta Magellan. Learn all about vultures—the gross things they do, what they eat, whether a turkey vulture gobbles, and more.

CPSIA information can be obtained at www.ICGtesting.com
Printed in the USA
BVOW10s0431260515

401583BV00001B/2/P